J
696
LI   Lillegard, Dee
     I can be a plumber

$12.60

| DATE | | | |
|---|---|---|---|
| JY 16 '92 | | | |
| DEC 13 '94 | | | |
| NOV 23 '96 | | | |
| JUL 27 '98 | | | |
| OCT 08 '98 | | | |
| FE 12 00 | | | |
| JE 26 00 | | | |
| AP 21 '03 | | | |
| AG 09 '08 | | | |
| N 23 '13 | | | |

© THE BAKER & TAYLOR CO.

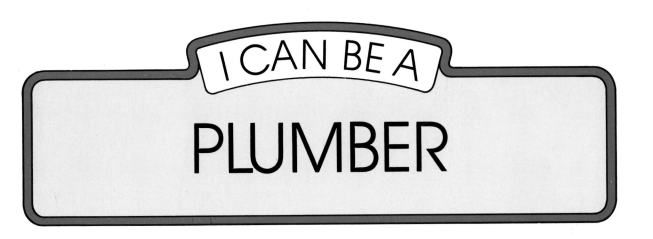

# I CAN BE A
# PLUMBER

By Dee Lillegard and Wayne Stoker

Prepared under the direction of Robert Hillerich, Ph.D.

 CHILDRENS PRESS ®

CHICAGO

Library of Congress Cataloging-in-Publication Data
Lillegard, Dee.

  I can be a plumber.

  Summary: Describes the training necessary to be a
plumber and the many kinds of work they do.
  1. Plumbers—Juvenile literature. 2. Plumbing—
Juvenile literature. [1. Plumbing—Vocational
guidance. 2. Vocational guidance. 3. Occupations]
I. Stoker, Wayne. II. Title.
TH6124.L55 1987   696'.1'023    86-30950
ISBN 0-516-01906-6

Childrens Press, Chicago
Copyright ©1987 by Regensteiner Publishing Enterprises, Inc.
All rights reserved. Published simultaneously in Canada.
Printed in the United States of America.
  2 3 4 5 6 7 8 9 10 R 96 95 94 93 92 91 90 89 88

# PICTURE DICTIONARY

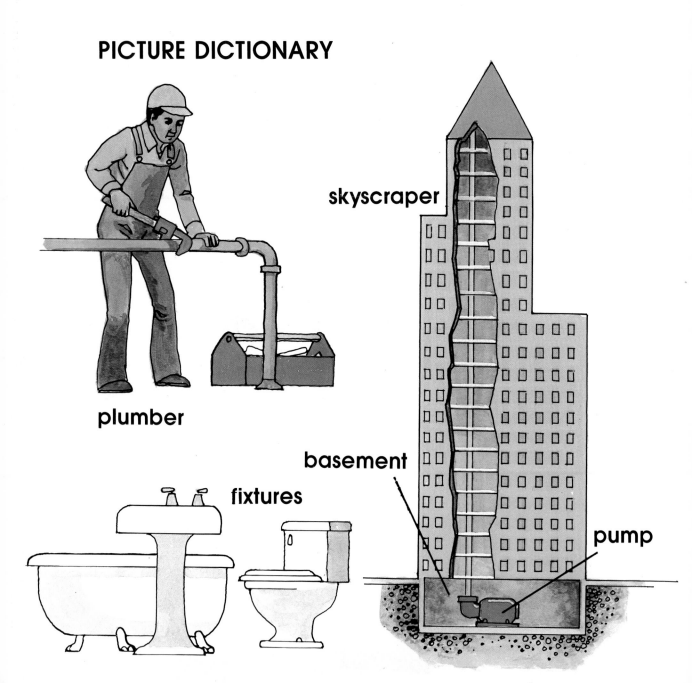

plumber

skyscraper

basement

pump

fixtures

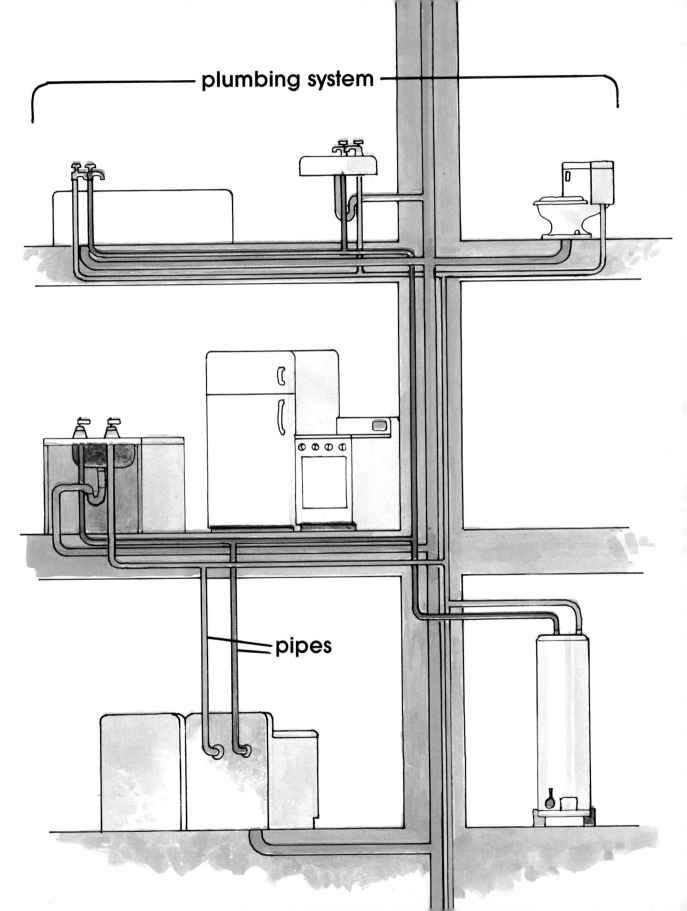

plumbing system

pipes

Beneath a bathroom floor you'll find a bathtub drain (above) and toilet and sink drains (below). The blue handles are shut-off valves for fresh hot and cold water. Right: Pipes beneath a sink. Below right: Pipes and water tanks in a basement.

Look around your home. Look around any modern building. You can't see what's hidden behind the walls and under the floors. You can only see a few parts of something that is very important—the plumbing system.

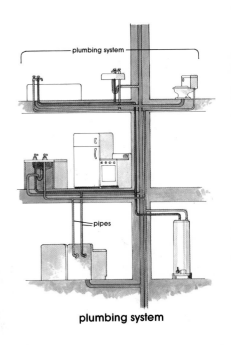

plumbing system

Every house and building has many pipes. Some of the pipes bring in clean water. Others carry out used water.

These hidden pipes go to *fixtures,* such as bathtubs, showers, and toilets. They go to dishwashers, clothes washers, and sinks.

Plumbers work with these important pipes

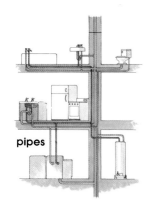

pipes

plumber

Wastewater that leaves our homes goes to a sewage treatment plant (left). After treatment, a technician tests the water for purity (right).

and fixtures. Every type of building—every house, school, hospital, and factory—depends on good plumbing. Clean water must come in

**fixtures**

7

through one system of
pipes. Used water must
go out through another.
The two must never mix.

The ancient Greeks
and Romans knew the
importance of clean
water. They used lead to
make their pipes. The
word plumber comes
from *plumbum,* the Latin
word for "lead."

Today, plumbers work
with pipes of brass,

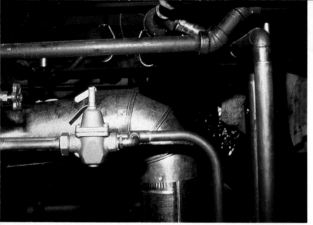

Top: Lead and copper pipes (left) and a brass pipe (right)
Bottom: Vinyl drain pipes (left) and clay drain pipes (right)

copper, and steel. They
may also work with glass,
plastic, tile, or concrete.
Many pipes today are
made of a strong
material called *polyvinyl*

Left: Cutting a pipe. Right: An apprentice plumber

*chloride* (PVC). Plumbers cut, bend, and join pipes to make plumbing systems.

Most plumbers start out as apprentices. They learn their trade on the job.

Apprentices learning to read mechanical drawings

Apprentice plumbers
learn how to use special
tools and materials. They
learn how to install pipes,
drains, and sewers. They
may also go to school to
study science,

Plumber and apprentice with all kinds of fixtures

mathematics, drafting, and blueprint reading.

Plumbers need to know how to join pipes together. They learn to measure accurately so the pipes will fit where they belong and never leak.

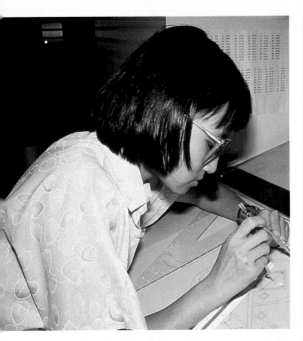

Left: "Drafting" is making an exact drawing of all the parts in a
building—including the plumbing system. Right: Cutting and threading
a pipe. "Threading" is putting grooves in a pipe so it can screw
in to another pipe.

Plumbers also figure
out water pressures. It is
important that there be
enough pressure to make
water run through the
fixtures. But too much
pressure can damage a
plumbing system.

13

Plumbers who complete their apprenticeship become journeymen. In some areas, they have to take state and local examinations to get a plumber's license.

After many years of experience, a skilled journeyman may

Laying out the plumbing system for a new building

become a master
plumber. Master
plumbers are trusted with
the most expensive
materials in the most
difficult situations.

Right: Plumbers have to be healthy and strong. Below: Installing a septic tank, a concrete tank that holds wastewater

A master plumber may have to develop a plumbing system that is not hidden. A plumbing system that can be seen must be artistically pleasing.

Plumbing is hard work, so plumbers must be in good physical condition. They have to lift heavy pipes and fixtures.

These are some of the parts that plumbers use to make our plumbing work.

Plumbers must be alert and careful. And they should enjoy working with their hands.

Left: Installing a sewer system for wastewater
Right: Laying drain pipes

On large plumbing
jobs, plumbers work in
pairs or groups. It is
important that they be
able to cooperate.

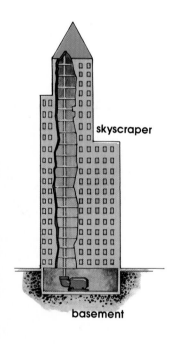

skyscraper

basement

Plumbers work both indoors and outside. They may work down in a basement or high up in a skyscraper. They must often work in small, cramped places.

Drafting the plans for a large building includes designing
a complicated system of pumps and pipes.

Did you ever wonder how water gets from ground level to the top floor of a tall building? That is the plumber's job. Plumbers use pumps to increase the water pressure. In very high buildings there may be many pumps on different floors. And there are lots of pipes! Without modern plumbing, we could not have skyscrapers.

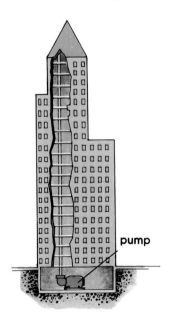

pump

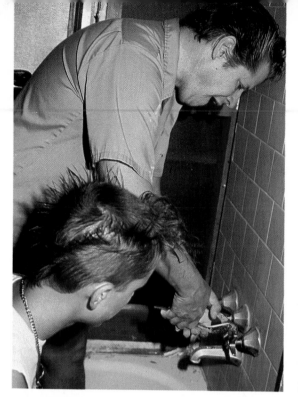

Making plumbing repairs

The plumbers' job is not done when plumbing systems are installed. These systems must be maintained. Plumbers are needed to make repairs, to thaw frozen pipes, and to clear clogged drains.

Many people throughout the world do not have plumbing in their homes. They get water from a village water supply (left) or from a lake, river, or stream (right).

Without good plumbing
to carry wastewater
away, unsanitary
conditions could cause
sickness and disease.

Adjusting a water-flow valve at a sewage treatment plant

After any disaster, plumbers have to work night and day. They must make sure all plumbing systems are repaired and water is safe to drink.

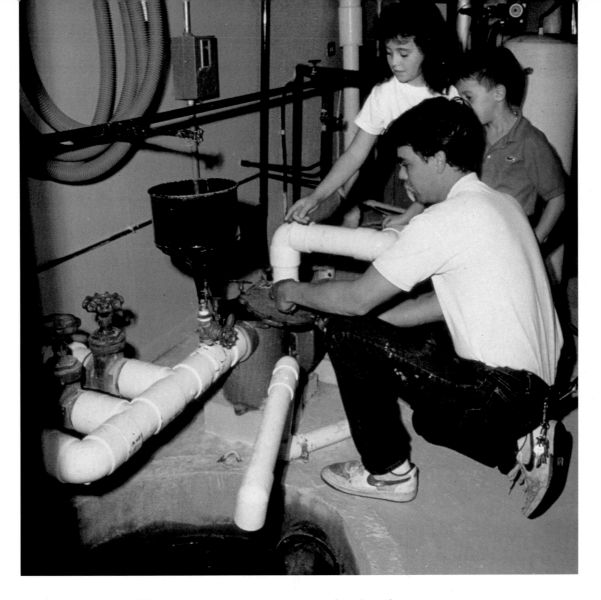

The plumber's job is a
challenge. The health
and comfort of many
people depend on the
plumber's work.

Not so many years ago,
people had to go to
outdoor bathrooms—in
wind, rain, and snow.
Because of modern
plumbing, we can have
bathrooms *inside* our
houses.

We can drink a glass
of cool water on a hot

The pleasures of plumbing: Fresh, clean water
at our fingertips and a warm, sudsy bath

summer day. We can
enjoy a warm bath on a
cold winter night. All we
have to do is turn on a
faucet. But we couldn't
do that without plumbers.

## WORDS YOU SHOULD KNOW

**apprentice** (uh • PREN • tiss)—someone who is learning a trade by working on the job with a more skilled person

**blueprint** (BLOO • print)—an architect's drawings of the plan for a building, showing the measurements of all its parts

**challenge** (CHAL • unj)—a hard job that is a test of someone's skills

**disaster** (dih • ZAS • ter)—a terrible happening that endangers people's lives, such as a flood or an explosion

**drafting** (DRAFT • ing)—drawing, especially drawing plans for a building

**faucet** (FOSS • it)—a spout out of which water flows when a handle is turned

**fixtures** (FIX • cherz)—useful objects that pipes take water to and from, such as sinks, toilets, and showers

**installed** (in • STAHLD)—fixed into place

**journeyman** (JER • nee • mun)—a person who has successfully completed an apprenticeship

**lead** (LED)—a metal used in batteries and construction materials. It is poisonous when eaten or drunk.

**plumbing system** (PLUM • ing SISS • tum)—all the pipes and the fixtures connected to them in a building

**polyvinyl chloride** (POL • ee • vy • nul KLORE • ide)—a hard, plastic-like material used to make rainclothes and pipes; also called PVC

**pump** (PUMP)—a device that mechanically pushes a liquid through pipes

**sewer** (SOO • er)—an underground place to which wastes and wastewater are piped

**skyscraper** (SKY • skray • per)—a very tall building. It has this name because the building seems to scrape the sky.

**unsanitary** (un • SAN • ih • teh • ree)—unhealthful; containing disease-causing germs

**water pressure** (WAW • ter PRESH • er)—the force with which water flows. Water that gushes out has high pressure; water that trickles has low pressure.

# INDEX

# PHOTO CREDITS

# ABOUT THE AUTHORS

Dee Lillegard (born Deanna Quintel) is the author of over two hundred published stories, poems, and puzzles for children, plus *Word Skills*, a series of high-interest grammar worktexts, and *September to September, Poems for All Year Round*, a teacher resource. In this series, she has written *I Can Be a Baker* and *I Can Be a Carpenter* and co-authored *I Can Be an Electrician* and *I Can Be a Welder*. Ms. Lillegard has also worked as a children's book editor and teaches writing for children in the San Francisco Bay Area. She is a native Californian.

Wayne McMurray Stoker is a Culinary Arts instructor at Laney Community College in Oakland, California. A tradesman at heart, he has been involved in the building and manufacturing trades all his life and cannot resist exploring what makes things work. In this series, he has co-authored *I Can Be an Electrician* and *I Can Be a Welder*. Having spent his early childhood in the rural South, where storytelling was a natural pastime, Mr. Stoker finds writing for children to be an enjoyable extension of his widely varied experience.